Poems That Inspire Contemplation

Michael L. Cunningham

VANTAGE PRESS
New York

FIRST EDITION

Published by Vantage Press, Inc.
516 West 34th Street, New York, New York 10001

Manufactured in the United States of America
ISBN: 0-533-11741-0

Library of Congress Catalog Card No.: 95-90862

0 9 8 7 6 5 4 3 2 1

Contents

Poems That Inspire Contemplation

A Poem

A poem should be
Thoughtful and incisive,
Evoke passions and emotions
Educate and enlighten.

A poem should be
Meaningful and poignant
Serious yet lighthearted
Believable and sincere.

A poem should arouse
Feelings deep within,
Have substance and value,
Awaken your consciousness,
Penetrate the cobwebs in your mind.

A poem should leave you
Pondering what you've read,
Analyzing its message
With interest and concern

A poem should
Stimulate and motivate
Encourage and comfort
Inspire and inform.

What is a poem?
A poem brings life into focus
From the viewpoint of the author.

Accomplishment

The beauty of success
Is the feeling it creates;
The ecstasy it delivers
Puts you on top of the world.

The effort that brought you
To your moment of elation,
Will not be soon forgotten
But remembered as a labor of love.

The confidence which is attained
From a successful endeavor,
Aids in the pursuit
Of your next undertaking.

Fresh with victory
Your ego is inflated;
Anything can be accomplished
If the same intensity is exerted.

Don't shortchange yourself
With an I'll-accept-whatever-happens attitude;
Dare to expose your ability
With an I-control-my-own-fate viewpoint.

The strength you will derive
Once success has come your way,
Will give your mind the inspiration
To seek out new challenges.

Allegiance

Faith is the substance of things hoped for
Evidence of things not yet seen,
The Lord believes in us;
Why can't we believe in Him?

Jesus paved the road
Down which we should travel;
Follow in His footsteps
And you won't be steered wrong.

God's grace is abundant
God's strength is His patience;
Let your belief in the Lord
Control the life you live.

Abide by the Lord's teachings
And your reward will be substantial;
God provides the support
To keep your life stabilized.

God promised us eternal life
If we hold tight to His word;
Place your faith in the Lord
And all your dreams will be recognized.

America

A cry of pain
A scream for help
Screeching tires of a speeding car
Loud sirens of police cars and ambulances
Profanity spewing from everywhere
The sound of gunfire; commonplace
Jet engines above us
Subway trains beneath us
Crime out of control
Life taken for granted
Homeless people abound
Prisons that don't rehabilitate
Rampant drug use.
Where are we?
"America, the Land of Opportunity!!"

Anger

In a fit of rage, reason disappears
And the mind does not hear;
What the brain tries to convey
The mind does not obey.

Reacting to the impulses sent
Out of anger and resentment,
Rationality and objectivity
Have given way to scorn and pity.

That mounting anger
Puts you in danger
Of making a choice
With anger in your voice
And hatred in your mind
Leaving all reasoning behind.

When you reach the edge
Instead of stepping off that ledge,
Step back and evaluate
Before it's too late,
And anger has caused you to act
Without considering the fact,
That decisions made in rage
Are rarely the ones we want to engage.

Keep your temper in check;
Don't let your life become a wreck,
From the animosity you possess
And making a judgment under duress.

Be patient and reflect
On what you're about to project;
It could have a long lasting effect;
Don't let it be something you'll regret.

Approach

Approach each day with anticipation,
Approach life enthusiastically,
Energize your mind with positive notions,
Envision total happiness.

Accept no one's proclamation
If they attempt to dampen your ambitions,
Your determination and devotion will prove invaluable
Should progress go awry,
As long as you stay focused
And believe in your ability,
The possibility to be victorious remains intact.

Success isn't always triumphing
At what you originally set out to do,
You gain immeasurably
From the process and involvement of any endeavor;
Don't take the position you didn't achieve;
Every bit of information gained is success,
Something good evolves from all encounters,
Be astute enough to recognize the possibilities.

We can always profit from our achievements
But sometimes learn more from disappointments,
None of us wants to come up short of our desire
But the strength derived from those situations builds
resolve;
We won't allow a temporary setback to prevent going
forward
For everything that happens aids our maturation;
Frustrations allow us to be more appreciative of
attainment

As they help develop the groundwork
To making us more grateful of accomplishments.

Don't let your objective
Cloud your mind
To all that is gained
Leading to your eventual outcome;
Realize the information gained;
Unravel the wealth of knowledge procured
From the involved process;
You gave yourself a challenge
And sought the data buried beneath the surface;
By committing to a project
And becoming more enlightened,
You have progressed and succeeded.

Keep the proper attitude
Plan to be prepared
Provide each day a positive outlook
And you will stay on course for tranquillity.

Belief

Trust in your convictions,
Be responsible for your actions;
Keep your mind clear of distractions
And do your best at all times.

The strength of your character
Will be severely tested,
By passing thoughts of doubt
That wish to hold you back.

Outside influences will attempt
To put a damper on your dreams;
Have the courage to brave the wave
Of all the doomsayers and naysayers.

Have patience in your quest;
Don't let urgency ruin the journey;
The old adage says
"Good things come to those who wait."
Time should be used wisely
But do not let it remove your motivation;
Time should not be a deterrent to success.

Follow through on your vision;
You know what you're capable of;
Determination and perseverance
Give you the right of way
Down the road to success.

Commit

God is always there for us;
He'll never abandon you;
There's no better friend
Than God Almighty.

If we give "Him" the opportunity
The Lord will guide us;
God is all we need
To be successful in life.

Our faith shouldn't waver;
Our trust should not fade;
There must not be any doubt
As to where our loyalties lie;
The Lord is always near;
Allow "Him" to navigate.

The struggles we face,
The tribulations we endure
God is aware;
God does not give us more than we can bear;
Just take the initiative
To place the Lord first.

Composure

Life is like an automobile,
Which we don't want to overload;
Keep it in proper balance
And it will guide you along smoothly.

Life will take you
As far as you want;
The onus is on you
To plot the course.

Life will grind to a halt
If you lose your desire;
It has to have motivation
To keep going strong.

Life will knock you down
And walk all over you,
If your mind is out of focus
And you have no direction.

The concept of life
Is bewildering to many;
Put life on notice
You're not going to give up.

Plan for the future
But don't forget the present;
You must survive today
To make it into tomorrow.

Concealment

The love that was buried
Behind the wall of protection,
Longed to be exposed
To the woman who entered his life.

He was cautious with his emotions
Not allowing them the freedom,
Of breaking through the wall
To discover the other side.

Maintaining this rigid structure
Appeared to keep him in control;
No one would notice the insecurity,
Which was abundant.

An experience not forgotten
Will forever remain a reminder,
Keeping the wall standing
Despite all attempts to break it down.

His heart severely crushed,
He can only go so far,
As to peek through the cracks
That the passage of time has created.

Unfortunately this man is destined
To live a lonely life,
Unless he summons the courage
To let love climb over that wall.

Confess

Admitting lack of knowledge is a success
If your mind is committed to growing;
Everyone requires assistance;
None of us has all the answers.

Never be afraid
To seek another's help;
You won't understand all situations
That invade and confront your life.

The only way to progress
Is to constantly thirst for information,
Drink from the pool of people
Who can drown you with the facts
You're desperately seeking.

You should not be uninformed
Because you're reluctant to ask;
Do you wish to remain at a standstill
Or gain the knowledge you desire?

Admit you don't know;
Don't let pride hold you back;
Pride should not be an impediment,
To keeping your mind unfamiliar
With what you want to comprehend.

Overcome ego;
Say, "I need help."
You'll find the answer you seek;
You'll be wiser intellectually;
What a price to pay!

Convictions

The beginning of success is to conceive;
Condition your mind to believe;
Ignore what others perceive;
Set your mind at ease;
Don't stop till you achieve.

You've got to have a strong will
To climb that very steep hill
Of doubt, which longs to kill
The dreams you wish to fulfill.

The struggle is worth the pain;
Never let your ambition wane;
Your effort will not be in vain;
Remember what you stand to gain.

By trying and doing your best
And not playing it close to the vest,
You put life to the test;
You've attained a measure of success.

Depression

Depression deflates the will
And de-energizes the body,
Takes over your mind
And leaves you mystified.

Depression destroys concentration,
Puts you on the defensive,
Causes your objectivity to disappear
And eliminates your hopes.

Depression is comparable to a virus
That spreads through the body;
If not gotten to in time,
The results can be very damaging.

Once depression takes control,
You become insecure,
Everything works against you,
You're positively negative.

Depression has its foundation,
On the perception you have of your life;
Gloss over the disappointments;
Dwell on the achievements.

Depression is defeatable
Once the symptoms are recognized;
Prioritize your life;
De-emphasize the mistakes;
Eliminate needless worry;
Take control of that which you're able to.

15

Take depression for a ride
Down the road to recovery;
When you've reached your destination,
Don't bother to look back;
Depression will be left behind;
You successfully made the climb
And your life is no longer in a bind.

Direction

God, let me use what You've given me
To help others along their journey;
Let me not selfishly think
Of only myself when others are in need.

God, give me the strength
To share with others
The blessings You've bestowed upon me;
Let me not refuse a cry for help
When You've graciously answered my prayers.

God, grant me the wisdom
To listen to others' thoughts and ideas
And understand their feelings and beliefs,
To impart knowledge I possess
To others who may voyage
Down a road I've already traveled.

God, don't let me forget
That it's better to give than it is to receive;
Give a little time;
Give of yourself;
Give hope to others,

But above all else, give your soul to the Lord.

Distress

The wounds on the body
May cause discomfort and anguish,
But a worse pain to confront
Is that which affects the heart.

Doctors and medicine may cure
The physical ailments of the flesh,
But where is the remedy
For the grief borne by the heart?

Accidents occur daily
And help is always summoned,
But when the spirit is disconsolate,
It has to find its own resolution.

The marks upon our skin will fade
As will the agony endured,
But when the heart is pierced,
The memory never leaves.

Don't Give Up

When things are bad and you can't cope,
Just when you feel you're at the end of your rope,
Money is gone and bills are due,
You're all depressed and feeling blue,
Life has just given you another hit,
Rethink your course but please don't quit.

We often think we're the only one
Doing all the struggling and having no fun,
But you must not give up the fight;
That dark cloud can turn to light;
Stay on course, though you have doubt,
Take that fear, and cast it out.

When life is on a downward slope,
Don't give up, there's always hope.
Change could be right around the bend;
Don't give up till you've reached the end,
The end that rewards the battle you fought,
The end that allows you to open your eyes and see
It was worth the effort, wouldn't you agree?

Dreams

Let us have dreams of achievement,
Dreams that push us forward,
Dreams that encourage progress,
Dreams that are far-reaching.

Don't put a limit on your dreams;
Never let anyone discourage your ambition,
Strive for that which may appear unattainable;
Stretch yourself to the perimeter of your mind,

If you can conceive it, the possibility is there.
Our imagination gives us the ideas,
Our knowledge and wisdom the ability to follow through.

There is a basis for that which may appear outlandish,
Dedication and determination our seeming
      encumbrance,
Any dream that causes you to evoke an effort, gains
You experience, gives you awareness, is a dream of
      substance.

Encouragement

Life isn't always what it seems;
Our struggles today will turn into faded memories;
The apparent hopelessness of our situation
Will be sources of encouragement down the road;
The inadequate feeling we may possess now
Will become a distant remembrance.

Don't ever give up on yourself;
Never lose your desire to succeed;
Look for a positive in all circumstances;
The Lord knows the strength of our character
Whatever our predicament may be;
The Lord will always see us through.

Endurance

Permit your spirits to remain high
Amid the disappointments of life;
Better days are ahead
Though the outlook may seem bleak.

The problems we encounter
Strengthen our ability
To deal with unpleasantness;
Each block along the way
Is a barrier to be overturned.

You're not always prepared
For all life's uncertainties;
Adjustments have to be made
But courage pilots your plane.

Life is not going to be easy
So take nothing for granted;
You will experience lows
But that allows the spirit to grow.

The darkness of your plight
Will soon turn to light;
If you use all your might
And don't give up the fight,
Everything will turn out right.

Existence

Don't let setbacks hold you down,
Gain strength from disappointments,
Keep the will to progress forward
Instead of giving in to adversity.

None of us is going to go through life
Unscathed from agony,
Everyone will have moments in their lives
When faith and confidence are tested.

Be tenacious in coping with strife,
Handle it with courage and aplomb,
No situation is so bleak
That we should lose our determination to continue.

All of life is a challenge
That we are more than capable of meeting,
The ability comes from our inner strength
Acquired through life's experiences
To not succumb to distractions and misfortune
Which attempt to overpower our resolve.

In a moment of crisis
It may seem impossible to survive misfortune;
That is a normal reaction
But don't accept that reaction as gospel;
Defeat the initial shock
By realizing life has only put an obstacle
In your path which can be overcome.

Keep in mind life is an ongoing education
And each event that occurs
Is a lesson to learn
To aid in the days that follow.

Advance through distresses and griefs
By becoming stronger and wiser
And accepting life's events as a growing process.

Eyes

Two pairs of eyes
Meeting in unison
Unable to look away—
The magic of the moment.

Words yet to be spoken,
Infatuation or lust,
Eyes still focused;
Feelings inside erupting.

Spirit of the soul
Can be read through the eyes,
Eyes still attached
Not missing a single thought.

These eyes unearthing
Passion they can't dispute,
Eyes not blinking
Mesmerized in flight.

Path of the eyes
Temporarily interrupted;
Eyes don't notice
The moment transcends obstacles.

The astonishment of their eyes
To the amazement of others,
Has them spellbound—
The power of the eyes.

Failure

Failure is not a crime
Nor is it a waste of time;
Failure is best used
As an incentive to push forward.

Failure is not a curse;
There are a lot of things worse;
Not succeeding at your attempt
Doesn't signal the end of the world.

Failure is a momentary setback;
Don't let it keep you off track;
Gain from the experience
And get a fresh start.

Failure should not cause despair
Or cause you to lose your desire;
If it's something you feel strongly about
Don't let it overpower your urge to achieve.

From the depths of failure
To the height of success,
It is the wise man who is not afraid to fail,
For he will learn far more
Than the one who never makes an effort.

Failure is not a disaster
It is not a sign to give up;
The outcome of your endeavor
Lies purely with your devotion.

Friends

Friends you can depend on
Are a rare breed;
They will stick with you through troubles
To help you find your way.

To keep a proper perspective
On your real friends,
Notice how they react
When adversity strikes.

True friends listen to your problems
And offer solutions;
They won't turn away
When understanding and assistance are necessary.

True friends can be relied upon
No matter the situation;
The tougher your predicament is
The more they'll want to help.

They will not lie to you
To enhance your ego;
Total honesty from them
Is what you expect.

True friends will not panic
Or take advantage of you,
When you're feeling down
And no one else is around.

To put it very simply
The friends you want most,
Are those who know you best
And won't question when you need them.

Friendship

The worth of friendship
Is found in honor,
The pledge of friendship
Is found in commitment,
The depth of friendship
Is found in devotion,
The quality of friendship
Is found in loyalty,
The value of friendship
Is found in integrity,
The importance of friendship
Is the camaraderie it provides,
The most significant aspect of friendship
Is it's based on mutual respect and admiration.

Happiness

Happiness is not difficult to find;
It's different for everyone
But we all can locate it;
The road to happiness
Can be narrow as a stream
Or wide as a river;
You control that disparity.

Riches and power are not essential for happiness;
Happiness can be a walk in the park,
A drive by the lake,
A quiet moment alone;
Happiness does not have to cost.

Happiness is kindness displayed and received,
Happiness is seeing your joy uplift someone else,
Happiness is sharing,
Happiness is helping others succeed,
Happiness is doing what you want, freely!

The road to happiness may lead to various destinations,
But the one place they all should intersect,
To be completely happy:
You must have peace of mind.

Heart (I)

The sun is the center of the universe;
The heart is the center of your soul;
Without the sun, there is no brightness;
Without sharing your heart, you are in the dark;
Without the sun, the Earth would be cold;
If you don't share your heart, you're left out in the cold;
All planets revolve around the sun;
All emotions revolve around your heart;
You could not live if there were no sun;
If you don't share your heart, you are missing out on life;
Getting too close to the sun can be fatal;
Sharing your heart can also be dramatic;
It can bring you tremendous joy as well as pain
But if you don't open it, you can't experience the feelings;
You can't touch the sun
But your heart can be touched,
The sun is an object that can stand alone
But the heart is meant to be shared, not closed to the
world.

Heart (II)

The heart is an instrument
That's so very fragile;
It doesn't take much
For it to be broken.

Time heals all wounds
Is a popular notion,
But the heart is so delicate
That's not always the case.

The heart is very sensitive
To everything that happens;
It's easier to forgive
But more difficult to forget.

A heart that has been broken
Is not easily mended;
It has to endure the pain
To overcome the hurt.

Your heart is the key
To all that takes place;
It enables you to enjoy
The beauty of life.

Everyone's heart is different
But there is one thing in common:
You have to share it
To reap the full benefits.

Honor

It is easy to be friendly and delightful
When everything is looking bright,
But will you have that same demeanor
When life takes a turn for the worse?
The true test of strength is adversity;
We all will face its wrath;
The ability to smile
Through those troubled times
Underscores your understanding of life.

We have to be cautious and sensible
When temptation comes knocking at our door;
Although we may not answer
Temptation never goes away;
Waiting for its opportunity
Temptation bides its time,
But if we are to be truly honorable
That desire will remain unquenched.

The virtues that are inherent
In those who survive the tests
Life so generously administers
Are at the backbone of adaptability;
These strengths are bred in faith
And the courage to challenge life head-on,
Knowing you're not going to win every battle
But nonetheless handling every setback with a grin,
There's no pretense about their integrity,
No question about their character.

It is these who are deserving of respect.

Knowledge

Arm yourself with knowledge
And you'll never be at a disadvantage,
Let your mind be a sponge
And soak up all the information you can.

Knowledge is power
It can make a difference in your life,
Knowledge gives the expertise
To comprehend the complexities of life.

Put knowledge to the test
Don't set boundaries on your mind,
Search for venues that will expand your potential,
You can't attain too much knowledge.

Develop the wisdom of your mind
Explore the depths of your soul,
Augment your life by engaging
In challenges that will benefit you mentally
As well as spiritually.

Don't restrict yourself to only one aspect of life.
Scrutinize the whole spectrum of thoughts, feelings, and
emotions,
Be wise in as many charges as possible,
The better versed you are
The better you will feel about yourself
And want to continue exploring and probing
To gain additional knowledge

If you possess enough knowledge
You will have a sense of accomplishment,
You will have something that can't be taken away,
You will be a more confident person,
You will better appreciate and understand life,
You will not be at the mercy of others,
You will control your own destiny,
And isn't that what we all want
To be in control of our own fate?

Let Go

The loneliness of heartbreak
Can devastate your life;
It causes sleepless nights
And culminates in depression;
Your heart doesn't want to accept
That the feeling won't be back.

The pain of withdrawal
That the heart suffers from,
Is not quickly forgotten
Nor easy to overcome.

The battle that goes on
Inside your mind
Keeps the fire burning
Long after the flame is out.

The emptiness you experience
Seems like a bottomless pit;
The feeling gets lower and lower
With no end in sight.

The road to recovery
Lies in confronting the situation;
Accept all the hurt
Don't deny the sorrow.

It's a slow and painful process
But in the end you'll succeed;
You'll have withstood the heartache;
You're ready to move on.

Life

Life takes many different twists and turns;
It involves consequences for actions
And sacrifices to achieve goals;
It's a constant struggle
To keep on the right path.

The hard lessons learned along the way
Shape the person that we become;
Each experience gives us wisdom
As to what we are about.

Everyone has troubles and problems,
A part of life which can't be avoided;
Not getting overwhelmed or consumed,
The ability to effectively handle them,
Emphasizes how strong your convictions to life are.

Handling new and different situations
Can change our perspective of life,
If we properly and honestly digest the information
That brought us to our eventual conclusion.

Not letting the past influence future reactions
To occasions similar albeit unrelated
Requires a strong mindset,
But if achieved,
Allows growth as an individual.

We are very ingenious people;
Everyone possesses intelligence;
Whether we use that ability in a positive fashion
Is part of our identity
And how we are perceived.

Given all that happens in our lives,
We should be able to cope with whatever arises,
As long as there are no preconceived notions
And our mind stays open to transformation.

Life's Mission

Life is an investment, manage it properly
Life is charity, make a contribution
Life involves risks, take them
Life is an obligation, comply with it
Life is a maze, master it
Life is an honor, uphold it
Life requires effort, exert yourself
Life is an expedition, travel it
Life needs an objective, devise one
Life is faith, don't lose it
Life is a battle, combat it
Life is pain, bear the burden
Life is your mission, complete it.

Living Life

Life brings us joy and pain;
It gives you strength and makes you weak;
Life is complicated but oh so easy;
Control and discipline will show you the way.

Life gives hope that all is not lost;
Life teaches lessons on how to live,
You must live life to gain experience,
The experience of which
Life's foundation is laid.

Life's difficulties are obstacles that shape our being;
Life's problems are nothing that can't be overcome,
Give life all you can and take heed
That the essence of life is the passion you evoke.

Lonely

Lonely is the man
Who has no friends,
No one to talk to
Just to pass the time of day.

Lonely is the man
Who has no one to confide in,
All his burdens
Being kept within.

Lonely is the man
Who cannot trust,
Suspicious of everyone
Who crosses his path.

Lonely is the man
Who cannot love,
Never experiencing the joy
Of sharing life with another.

Lonely is the man
Who thinks only of himself,
Not willing to acknowledge
The existence of others.

Lonely is the man
Who doesn't know God,
Ultimately he will find company
Among the throngs of those in Hell.

Love

Love grants peace and serenity,
Love depends on trust;
Trust is built on faith;
Faith gives you hope;
Hope breeds ambition;
Ambition comes from our dreams;
Dreams are desires;
Desires become goals;
Goals encourage us to strive and give life our best;
Once we have love, everything else falls in place.

Method

Untap the hidden abilities
Lying dormant deep in your brain;
Unleash that vast potential
Tied up amid the confusion
Which encompasses your mind.

Challenge the capacity of your mind;
Bring that creativity to the forefront;
Strive to surpass the limitations
Set forth by your own inhibitions.

The toughest projects to overcome;
The doubts and fears of failure,
Tracks that must be crossed
If you are to execute your destiny.

Trust the ability you possess;
Stretch your mind to the brink of exhaustion;
If you lose yourself in knowledge
You'll find the key to life.

Overwhelmed

I've fallen in love;
This can't be happening;
Somebody help me please
And set my mind at ease.

How can I break this spell
That has encompassed my body?
Somebody, anybody, give me a clue;
I don't know what the hell to do.

My heart is aching
And my stomach feels empty;
I let my guard down;
Is it really love I've found?

Try as I might
I had no luck;
The feeling would not leave;
Was I really lovestruck?

Doctor Doctor, give me a drug;
I've been bitten by the love bug;
The cure is simple
For your disease;
Just ask her
Will you marry me, please?

You'll share your life
With the lady you love,
Living happily ever after
And thanking the Lord above.

Past

The past is history;
The future is a mystery;
Don't live what has happened;
Don't fear what is to come.

History has its value
But keep it in proper perspective;
Don't penalize life from the knowledge
Which the past has etched in your mind.

The future is where your thoughts should be;
Focus on what lies ahead;
You can't prepare for the past;
Once it's gone, it's gone.

Pick out from the past
What you can use to build a future;
All other events are informational
Meant to inform, not block your progress.

One day your future
Will eventually become the past;
Take full advantage of the opportunity
To remember it fondly, not regretfully.

Prepare

Discipline is a necessary ingredient
To be a success in life;
Mix it in with determination and commitment
Along with experience, knowledge, and logic.

Discipline yourself not to be distracted;
Commit yourself to whatever needs to be done;
Determine to yourself not to give up;
Refuse to accept defeat.

Experience teaches us we are not as smart
As we would like to believe;
Use experience as a guide
To lead us were we need to go
And learn what we need to know.

Combine your knowledge with logic
To plan a course of action
Which rationally maps out a trail
To what you hope to accomplish.

Success is not totally dependent
On possessing all those attributes,
But use them as a pathfinder
When plotting your method of attack.

Progress

Dreams of the future,
Memories of the past,
Learn from history
And concentrate on the present.

The past is your escort
To forge you ahead;
Let those experiences
Help blaze a new trail.

Bring your life into view
By profiting from the teachings
Which the past has taught us;
Let your mind breathe in
The air of knowledge.

Every day there is a message
Waiting to be answered;
Pick up the phone
And dial in to life.

We must not lose sight;
Don't blind yourself to life,
Open your eyes to the prospects
Waiting to be seen and conquered.

Respectful

All the good that happens in life
Is a gift from God,
Never think you have accomplished anything without
help
God makes all things possible.

God provides the strength
To allow you to achieve your goals,
God's word is the inspiration
To keeping you on the straight path.

God's teachings remind us
Not to give up hope,
Faith and patience are key elements
To understanding the works of the Lord.

God will not leave you unfamiliar
If you're sincere in adopting His preachings,
Devote the time,
Pray for awareness,
Trust in the Lord,
And God will shine the light.

God knows we aren't perfect
But doesn't hold that against us,
God bestows blessings to one and all,
The choice is yours to accept them.

God sacrificed His son
To give us a chance at eternal life,
That demonstration of His love
Should move us to be loyal and faithful.

Respect the Lord's words,
Allow your life to be guided by truth,
Keep God near to your heart
And you shall be rewarded.

Runaway

Lost and alone
A scary thought,
The frightened child
Not knowing whom to trust.

Searching for direction,
Which way is right?
No one to turn to
In your time of need.

People walking past
As you helplessly watch,
Rushing about their business
Not noticing your plight.

Finally the dreaded tears
Stream down your cheeks;
Not a friendly face
Has come to your rescue.

Trying to be brave
You wipe away the tears,
Telling yourself
I'm in control.

But as night arrives
And you've made no progress,
That brave front
Has given way to fear.

Fear of the unknown,
Fear of the dark,
Fear that you'll never
Make it back home.

That home you left
Vowing never to return,
Home sweet home,
That's where you belong.

Sharing

Feelings intense,
Emotions within exploding,
Affection and passion undeniable,
This wasn't infatuation
Or a sexual urge;
Love had invaded his heart.

He was incapable of disguising
The excitement and exhilaration
She deposited into his life;
His face displayed
A look of admiration
Whenever her name was mentioned.

Nary a discouraging word
Could be heard when he spoke
About the woman who awakened his consciousness;
He was lost in love
And not looking to be found,
Such ecstasy he was under.

He exposed his soul
And knocked down the wall
That had hidden his emotions from the world;
She stormed his life;
He threw caution to the wind
And love was blown in his direction.

Following his heart
Made his life complete;
The story could now be concluded;
She fulfilled the need
He thought unnecessary,
He had a love with whom to share his life.

Sincerity

A man speaks his mind
With the eloquence of an orator,
But the words have no value
Unless they are genuine and virtuous.

The true man is a mountain
Unable to be easily conquered,
Sensitive to others' feelings
Not afraid of intimidation,
Admitting to mistakes and imperfections
And benefiting from criticisms that have merit.

Nothing is secret; he's not a phony,
No disguises or deceit,
Forthright and direct
There's no doubt about his position.

His words are not shrouded in mystery;
His self-assurance gives him the impetus
To choose the path he believes is correct
Not worrying about how it's perceived.

Take a person who is sincere
And wade through their shortcomings;
Accept and understand,
If they recognize the same in you;
You've found a friend.

Solving the Puzzle

The wonderment of life
Is the simplicity it involves;
The amazement of life
Is not everyone understands it.

It's not so complicated
You must be a genius,
Someone of small intellect
Could comprehend its meaning.

We all have the capability
To be successful in life;
You have to persevere the rough times
And push onward and ahead.

Life is a constant battle
From others and from within,
But you must stay focused
On the ultimate objective.

The irony of it all
Is we are our own worst enemies;
We can't seem to fathom
That the good life is ahead of us.

The beginning of knowledge
Is first accepting you don't know it all;
Once accomplished,
Progress in our lives may begin.

Our "needs" can be satisfied;
It's the "wants" that cause us trouble,
Distinguishing the difference in those two
Is not easily attained,
But once achieved,
Is a step in the right direction.

Our life can be easier
If our priorities are in place,
Knowing what's really important
Puts you on the right path.

Streets

Walking through the night, oblivious to the
surroundings,
Ignoring the sights and sounds that cause people to fear,
Stepping over drunks passed out in my path,
Just barely noticing prostitutes plying their trade,
Disregarding addicts administering the needle to their
arms,
Passing a police car, barely escaping its speeding path,
Turning a deaf ear to the beggars on my route
Who ask for help and curse as you depart,
The flash of gunshots lighting the sky,
Drug dealers all around for those in need,
Boarded-up houses and deserted buildings,
Havens for those who live for crime,
Stripped and deserted cars everywhere you turn,
Car alarms going off but no one noticing,
A fight on one side of the street,
A loud argument on the other,
Day or night
The time is really irrelevant;
These are the streets I have become accustomed to.

Succeeding

Always doing your best
Being true to those around you
Keeping focused on your goal
Analyzing and understanding
Looking ahead and not being inhibited
Using dreams to keep going
Not forgetting friends
Attending to details
Not afraid to take a chance
Throwing caution out the window
Stepping over defeat
Staying honest and true to yourself
Looking to heaven above
Living life to its fullest
Accepting setbacks with a smile and keeping the will to
go on
Overcoming struggles that seek to impede your progress
Striving through pressure, pain, and stress
That is success.

Success (I)

Success is the power of your mind
Envisioning and wanting to consummate
Dreams brought to fruition
Through desires, determination, and competence.

Desires and dreams can overcome fear and doubt;
The struggle will be rewarded;
Disappointments should not be a detriment
To triumph at your selected objective.

Benefit from those encounters;
Develop a stronger mentality;
Pressure yourself forward;
Don't dwell on an ill-fated endeavor.

Don't doubt yourself because of fear;
Don't let fear give you doubt;
Success is bred in overcoming those inhibitions
And challenging the control they hold.

When negativity starts brewing
Unplug that concept from your mind;
The plan you bought for success
Was sold with positive thinking.

The justice in succeeding
Is the exhilaration you will gain;
You made the right decision;
It was worth all the pain.

Success (II)

Success is something we've all enjoyed
Be it publicly or privately;
It fills you with pride and dignity
Increases your confidence and feeds your ego.

Success can be measured
In a variety of different ways.
It depends on where you started
And how difficult the effort was.

Being successful at a task
Might be considered minor to others;
Don't let that dishearten you;
Let yourself feel proud;
Revel in the feat you've accomplished
And prepare to leap the next hurdle.

Success is similar to love
In that it has a definite meaning,
But varies with the individual
As to what it means to them.

By what standards should we be judged?
How should success genuinely be gauged?
It can be simple as children saying no to drugs and sex
Or an event as glorious as winning a Nobel Peace Prize,
Each development is a success
With an enormous gap between the two;
There is no easy answer
To pinning down success precisely.

Success is really relative;
It's the opinion you have of yourself;
If you're happy with your life,
If you have your self-esteem,
You have attained success
Regardless of society's determination.

The First Time

The young girl seeks answers
On what to expect;
The young man anxiously awaits
His moment of conquest.

Young girl wanting to be an adult,
This is the way she chooses;
Young man wants some respect
From the friends he associates with.

Not wanting to be a prude
Young girl gives in to pressure;
Not wanting to be ridiculed
Young man claims he's done it.

The time has arrived
To follow through on plans,
But at that sacred moment
Both lose control.

Young girl weeps
Unsure of herself,
Young man panics
Trying to remain cool.

Neither was prepared
For that special occasion,
Their first virgin experience
Not remembered fondly.

Next time will be different
For the young man and girl,
But they will forever relive
That first failed attempt at love.

The Mind

Let your mind lead your journey
To depths and heights thought unreachable,
Challenges that eagerly await us
Testing the strength of our will.

Let your mind reach its potential;
Create the emphasis to push it further;
Never let doubt deter the mission;
Don't close the door to a possible victory.

Give your mind the power of positive thinking;
Believe in your ability to attain your objective;
Keep your mind active to avoid stagnation;
Let your mind wander through unconventional territory.

The mind possesses knowledge
Which will always remain hidden,
If we let our imagination die
And don't seek new adventures.

The Process

A baby is born, harmless and pure
Totally oblivious of what lies ahead,
Fragile and tender, depending on others,
Just a picture of innocence crying for attention
Hoping that someone answers its needs.

The first step taken, a special moment
But who is the proudest, parent or child?
We wait for the day when that first word is spoken
Knowing that's the beginning of more to come.

The baby has evolved into a small child
Eager to absorb everything in its path,
Full of questions and endless energy
Looking to you to satisfy its wants;
Mischief or happiness, which will it be;
To a child, there is no difference.

A teenager now, the world is much different;
Then dependence on you begins to wane,
Not because the need isn't there;
It is time for them to grow and experience for
themselves;
The pains of being a parent begin to magnify
As their maturity level begins to increase.

Leaving home now,
The day you've been waiting for,
Emotions running from sadness to joy;
However when that moment arrives
You're never quite prepared.

Although they are gone
The worry and concerns never leave;
All you can hope is the lessons were learned
And you guided them right
And try to let go
Knowing you did your best.

And when your children
Reminisce on their upbringing,
If they say "I may not have always agreed with the
decisions made
But my parents cared and were always there for me,"
Consider it a job well done.

Thoughts

Good thoughts are the glue
With which we hold ourselves together;
Having a positive attitude
Helps avoid the throes of depression;
Good thoughts build strength in character
And make the body feel good all over;
Forward thinking tips the scale in your favor
And keeps your mind away from adversity;
Good thoughts can make our darkest moments bearable
And give the power to overcome distractions.
If everyone had good thoughts
We would all be winners
And there would be no battles to wage.

The evidence is pretty obvious;
Good thoughts are not overflowing
But that mustn't dictate our thinking;
Inundate your life with good thoughts,
Spread the wealth to all who'll listen
And maybe a change in thinking patterns will develop;
Let good thoughts abound always in your mind
And your life will be much easier to handle.

Transition

As the years continue to pass
We should gain a better focus,
And become wiser from having lived
Through the troubled times behind.

We must often suffer
In order to move ahead;
Understanding life will remain a battle
Which we cannot escape.

Every event that occurs
Has a definite purpose;
Pay attention to your life;
Don't overlook any detail;
Consider the impact
Of your every action.

The only absolute
Is we will all depart this Earth;
All that takes place before then
Is how you will be remembered.

Troubles

Troubles are life's building blocks
Piled one on top of the other;
When the stack gets too high
It all comes crashing down.

Troubles test the strength of your will;
Use courage to brave and patience to handle them,
Logic to understand
And with faith they will disappear.

As troubles attempt to overtake your life,
Use your strength to fight,
And your ability to defeat them;
Have the confidence there is always hope
That better days are ahead.

Troubles are tiny pebbles
Which ignored grow into boulders,
Acknowledge them as soon as possible;
Don't let your life get bulldozed
By problems not addressed.

Undeniable

Madly in love
The two were inseparable;
They could not be any closer
If they were Siamese twins.

He spoke of her glowingly,
She talked about him endlessly;
There wasn't any doubt
Of their genuine sincerity.

Whenever they were apart
The love in their hearts,
Connected them together
Whatever the distance.

Although they missed one another
They were never alone,
Their hearts were as one
Feeling each other's ecstasy.

The passion between them
Was beyond description;
It was so utterly perfect
No one would believe it.

Honesty and trust
Were never issues,
The true love they shared
Could come only from total commitment.

The strength of their love
Could not be overpowered;
Their undeniable love
Can weather any storm.

What the World Needs

The world needs compassion and empathy
A bit more generosity and a lot less selfishness
More appreciation for the beauty of life
Less of an "only the strong survive" attitude
More understanding and awareness
Less prejudice and discrimination
More love and sensitivity
Less hate and malevolence
Thinking of others more than ourselves
Assisting those in distress rather than ignoring their
dilemma
Respect and concern for your fellow man.
The world needs more people with faith, vision, and
optimism
The strength, capacity, and ability to cope
Rather than the perception that we're at the end of our
rope
And there is no reason to hope.

Winner

If you give your best effort
But come up short
You are a winner;
By extending yourself to give all you have
You have prevailed
In spite of the outcome.

The mindset of a champion
Is one of supreme confidence;
The thought of not succeeding
Never enters the mind.

Reality of life says defeats will come;
A champion doesn't dwell on them
Nor doubts his own ability,
He accepts that it occurred
And becomes more determined to win.

A winner envisions his successes
Long before they ever happen,
Being mentally prepared for the occasion
When that moment arrives.

The strength of your character
Is reflected in the attitude
You have toward life
And in winning and losing.

A winner is persistent
Always looking for an edge;
To win you have to learn
From everything that happens.

Put life on notice
Nothing will hold you back;
You'll challenge every obstacle
And dissect every problem;
Leap every hurdle
And bury all disappointments;
In the game of life
You will be a winner.